D0801810

Sauces, Preserves & Liqueurs

The Taunton Press

ACADEMIA BARILLA
AMBASSADOR OF ITALIAN GASTRONOMY
THROUGHOUT THE WORLD

Academia Barilla is a global movement toward the protection, development and promotion of authentic regional Italian culture and cuisine.
With the concept of Food as Culture at our core, Academia Barilla offers a 360° view of Italy. Our comprehensive approach includes:

- a state-of-the-art culinary center in Parma, Italy;
- gourmet travel programs and hands-on cooking classes;
- the world's largest Italian gastronomic library and historic menu collection;
- a portfolio of premium artisan food products;
- global culinary certification programs;
- custom corporate services and training;
- team building activities;
- and a vast assortment of Italian cookbooks.

Thank you and we look forward to welcoming you in Italy soon!

CONTENTS

EDITED BY
ACADEMIA BARILLA

TEXT BY
MARIAGRAZIA VILLA

PHOTOGRAPHS
ALBERTO ROSSI

ACADEMIA BARILLA EDITORIAL COORDINATION
CHATO MORANDI
ILARIA ROSSI
REBECCA PICKRELL

RECIPES BY
CHEF MARIO GRAZIA
CHEF LUCA ZANGA

GRAPHIC DESIGN
PAOLA PIACCO

Mayonnaise: one of the sauces which serve the french in place of a state religion.

AMBROSE BIERCE, *THE DEVIL'S DICTIONARY*, 1911

SAUCES:

There is no cuisine in the world so tied to the idea of creating a "taste of home" as that of Italy. Small, tasty treasures, such as sauces and preserves, fill Italian kitchens from north to south. Made by hand from homegrown fruits and vegetables, often with the help of the whole family, these sauces and preserves are imbued with creativity, care, affection and the spirit of sharing. They are the embodiment of a busy, aromatic kitchen, one full of flavors, conversation and memories.

In this book, Academia Barilla, an international center dedicated to the promotion of Italian cuisine, has selected 40 traditional Italian recipes for sweet and savory sauces and preserves. For what would a dish be without its accompanying sauce? A sauce, after all, plays a fundamental role in the success of any dish, bringing out its essential flavors, from appetizers to desserts. It acts in combination with the food it accompanies to provide pleasure in every bite. The word *salsa* is derived from the Latin *salsus*, or "salted." In the kitchens of ancient Rome, garum, the liquid obtained from the long maceration of fish entrails (with herbs and salt), was a characteristic sauce. Needless to say, it was salty… and robust.

The history of Italian gastronomy, however, has also included many sauces created to dampen flavors deemed too intense, such as creamy,

HARMONIOUS INGREDIENTS

vegetable-based sauces used to round out the taste of meat preserved in brine. This diversity of sauces helped establish the reputation of Italian food throughout Europe during the Renaissance. Sauces were born out of necessity, used by creative chefs of the court as marinades or when roasting. Often based on simple ingredients, they became, when married, more than the sum of their parts. One of the country's most famous sauces, the tomato sauce, was created in Naples between the late seventeenth and early eighteenth centuries. With the tomato imported from the New World two centuries earlier, the rich red pulp of the tomato sauce first accompanied spaghetti, then pizza, an invention whose success would have been unthinkable without this red gold.

In the twentieth century, the art of sauces continued to be perfected, and Italian chefs were being spurred on by futurists such as poet Filippo Tommaso Marinetti, who urged cooks to do away with tradition in favor of "inventing something new at all costs, even if judged to be crazy." (In 1920, he proposed accompanying *zampone* [pig's trotters] of Modena with a fragrant broth of cologne and coffee.) This kind of experimental climate set the stage for some fantastic and unusual combinations, with often surprising, and delicious, results.

SAVORY RED SAUCE

Preparation time: 15 minutes   Cooking time: 2 hours   Difficulty: easy

4 SERVINGS

2 1/4 lbs. (1 kg) **cherry tomatoes**
1 tbsp. (20 g) **tomato paste**
5 oz. (150 g) **onion**, *or about 1 medium*
3 1/2 oz. (100 g) **carrot**
2 1/2 oz. (70 g) **celery**
2 oz. (50 g) **bell peppers**

2 cloves **garlic**
1 tsp. **chopped parsley**
1 bunch (20 g) **basil**
2 tbsp. (30 ml) **extra-virgin olive oil**
Salt and pepper *to taste*
Crushed red pepper flakes *to taste*

Peel the cherry tomatoes and remove the seeds, then quarter tomatoes. Chop the onion, carrot, celery, pepper, and garlic. Heat the oil in a frying pan over medium and gently fry the chopped vegetables until golden. When they have softened, add the parsley, basil, and crushed red pepper. Cook 2 minutes, then add the cherry tomatoes and tomato paste. Season with salt and pepper. Cook over low heat for about 2 hours, stirring occasionally.
After 2 hours, adjust the seasoning, adding a little salt and more red pepper flakes if necessary.

TOMATO PESTO
PANTELLERIA-STYLE

Preparation time: 15 minutes   Cooking time: 10 minutes   Difficulty: easy

4 SERVINGS

18 oz. (500 g) **tomatoes**, *or about 5 medium*
4 cloves **garlic** *peeled*
8 **basil leaves**
1 **fresh mint leaf**
1/4 cup (50 ml) **extra-virgin olive oil**
1 **chile pepper**, *chopped*
1 sprig **fresh oregano**
Salt *to taste*

Rinse tomatoes, carefully remove stems, and cut very shallow Xs into bottoms.
Bring a large pot of water to a boil. Blanch tomatoes in boiling water for 30
seconds. Remove tomatoes and put them in a bowl of cold water. Peel and
quarter the tomatoes, then rinse again, remove seeds and crush the tomatoes
with your hands to remove all the liquid.
With a mortar and pestle, crush the garlic, basil, and mint. Put all ingredients
in a pan, and add olive oil, chile pepper, oregano, and salt to taste.
Cook 10 minutes, stirring often.

SALMORIGLIO

Preparation time: 5 minutes   Cooking time: 3 minutes   Difficulty: easy

4-6 SERVINGS

1/2 cup plus 2 tbsp. (150 ml) **extra-virgin olive oil**
1/3 cup (80 ml) **hot water**
Juice of 2 **lemons**
1/3 cup (20 g) **chopped parsley**
1 clove **garlic**, *finely chopped*
1 tbsp. **dried oregano**
Salt and pepper *to taste*

With a fork, mix olive oil and hot water, gradually adding lemon juice, parsley, garlic, oregano, salt, and pepper. When the sauce is well emulsified and homogeneous, cook it in a bain-marie (hot water bath) or in a heatproof bowl set over a saucepan of simmering water for 3 minutes.
Use sauce as a condiment for grilled-fish dishes.

CAPER SAUCE

Preparation time: 10 minutes   *Difficulty: easy*

4 SERVINGS

3 oz. (80 g) **salted capers**
4 **anchovy fillets**
2 cloves **garlic**, *peeled*
3 1/2 tbsp. (50 ml) **extra-virgin olive oil**
Juice of 1 **lemon**
Salt and pepper *to taste*

Rinse capers and anchovy fillets. Halve garlic cloves lengthwise and remove the green sprout if present.

In a blender, purée capers, anchovies, garlic, and about 1 tablespoon of olive oil. Transfer to a bowl and drizzle in remaining oil, whisking constantly to form a thick sauce (if mixture is too thick, add a tablespoon of water). Whisk in lemon juice, and season with salt and pepper.

To make this sauce less pungent, you can replace the anchovy fillets with the same amount of tuna. Caper sauce is ideal as a seasoning for fish-based dishes.

WALNUT SAUCE

Preparation time: 15 minutes   Difficulty: easy

6 SERVINGS

15 *walnuts*
4 *cloves* **garlic**
2 oz. (50 g) **bread**
Milk
Salt and pepper *to taste*
Heavy cream *to taste*

Tear bread into very small pieces. In a bowl, soak them in enough milk that
bread will absorb it all (at least 1/4 cup). Shell walnuts and peel garlic.
Crush together using a mortar and pestle, or use a blender. Combine with
the bread soaked in milk and mix well.
Add salt and pepper to taste.
Just before serving, add cream (at room temperature) to taste.
Walnut sauce is ideal for pasta or ravioli.

OLIVE SAUCE

Preparation time: 8 minutes   Cooking time: 2 minutes   Difficulty: easy

4 SERVINGS

1/4 cup (60 g) **extra-virgin olive oil**
2 cloves **garlic**, *peeled and green sprouts removed*
1 cup (200 g) **pitted black olives**
Fresh parsley, *chopped, to taste*
3 tbsp. (40 g) **tomato purée** *(optional)*
Salt and pepper *to taste*

Heat the oil in a pan. Crush one of the cloves of garlic and leave the other whole. Cook them both in the oil, covered, over low heat for 3 to 4 minutes. Cut olives into small pieces and add to the pan. Cook a few minutes more, then remove garlic and add chopped parsley (or other herbs).
Season with salt and pepper.
To vary the flavor, substitute marjoram or oregano for the parsley (or use all the herbs together), or add a little tomato purée (if purée is added, cook sauce for an additional 10 minutes).
Olive sauce is delicious spread on toasts, for bruschetta, or served with farfalle or other short pastas.

HONEY-MUSTARD SAUCE

Preparation time: 10 minutes   Cooking time: 5 minutes
Resting time: 2 hours   Difficulty: easy

4 SERVINGS

3/4 cup (250 g) **honey**
3 oz. (80 g) **walnut pieces**
1 tbsp. (10 g) **mustard powder**
2 tbsp. (30 ml) **vegetable broth**

In a food processor, using the S-blade (or using a mortar and pestle), finely chop the walnuts. Heat the broth, then whisk in the mustard powder until it dissolves. Heat the honey in a small saucepan. When it is lukewarm, pour it and the broth mixture into the mortar (or food processor) with the walnuts, mixing it well. Remove to a serving bowl and let the sauce rest for 2 hours before using. Honey-mustard sauce pairs well with chicken breasts.

HORSERADISH SAUCE

Preparation time: 20 minutes   Difficulty: easy

4 SERVINGS

5 oz. (150 g) **horseradish root**
1 **tart apple** (such as Reinette or Granny Smith)
1 tsp. **sugar**
2 tbsp. (30 ml) **extra-virgin olive oil**
1/3 cup (80 ml) **white wine vinegar**
Salt to taste

Peel and grate the horseradish root, then add a pinch of salt and the sugar.
Peel and grate the apple and add it to the horseradish in a bowl.
Add the vinegar and oil to the horseradish-apple mixture and stir until
a sauce forms.
Serve with grilled fish, such as salmon, or with steak.

TOMATO PURÉE

Preparation time: 1 hour   *Difficulty: easy*

MAKES ABOUT 1 LB. 10 OZ. (750 G) PURÉE

2 lbs. (1 kg) **tomatoes**, *preferably San Marzano*

Rinse tomatoes, carefully remove stems, and cut very shallow Xs into bottoms. Bring a large pot of water to a boil. Blanch tomatoes in boiling water for 30 seconds. Remove tomatoes and put them in a bowl of cold water. Press tomatoes through a sieve (or use a food mill) to remove the skins and seeds. Let cool; then refrigerate in nonreactive containers for up to 5 days or freeze for up to a year. You can also can the purée for long-term use by following the instructions on page 34.

MAYONNAISE

Preparation time: 20 minutes   Difficulty: easy

MAKES ABOUT 1 1/2 CUPS

2 *egg yolks*
1 1/3 cups (330 ml) *olive oil or peanut oil*
1 tbsp. *white vinegar* or lemon juice
3/4 tsp. *salt*, or to taste

Combine egg yolks and salt in a medium bowl.
Vigorously whisk in about half of the oil in a slow stream (the mayonnaise will
have a more distinctive flavor if you use olive oil rather than peanut oil) until the
mayonnaise begins to thicken (or use an immersion blender). Whisk in the lemon
juice or vinegar, and continue to whisk in remaining oil in a slow stream until
mayonnaise is desired consistency.
If necessary, adjust the seasoning by adding more salt, vinegar or lemon juice.
Cover and keep refrigerated.

RICH GREEN SAUCE

Preparation time: 10 minutes   Difficulty: easy

4 SERVINGS

2 tbsp. (150 g) **fresh parsley**
2 oz. (50 g) **fresh breadcrumbs** *from about 2 slices soft white bread*
1 clove **garlic**
1 tsp. **capers**
1 **anchovy fillet**
1 **hard-cooked egg**
White vinegar *to taste*
Extra-virgin olive oil *to taste*
Salt

Soak breadcrumbs in just enough vinegar to saturate them. When breadcrumbs are saturated and soft, drain them in a fine-mesh sieve, pressing on them to remove excess moisture, and set aside. Rinse and dry the parsley, then finely chop it immediately before using, so that it will not acquire a strong bitter taste. Add the whole clove of garlic and the parsley to the strained breadcrumbs. If you prefer a stronger flavor, mince the garlic and stir it into the breadcrumbs with the parsley. If not, add the clove whole but remove it just before serving. Chop the capers, the hard-cooked egg and the anchovy, then combine with the breadcrumb mixture. Add oil and vinegar to taste, adding enough oil to cover the sauce. Add salt to taste.
The rich green sauce is the ideal accompaniment for braised meats.

SIMPLE GREEN SAUCE

Preparation time: 20 minutes   Difficulty: easy

4 SERVINGS

1 bunch **parsley**
1 **day-old white roll**
2 cloves **garlic**
2 tbsp. (100 ml) **extra-virgin olive oil**
1/3 cup (50 ml) **white wine vinegar**
Salt *to taste*

Remove the crust from the roll, crumble the roll, and soak the breadcrumbs in
vinegar until they are saturated. Lightly press out excess vinegar from
breadcrumbs. Rinse the parsley, removing the stalks, and peel the garlic.
In a food processor or blender, blend all the ingredients with the oil.
Add salt to taste and cover the sauce with oil to preserve it.
Serve with braised meats and grilled or roasted fish.

PRESERVED TOMATOES

Preparation time: 1 hour   Difficulty: easy

4 SERVINGS

2.2 lbs (1 kg) **tomatoes**, *preferably San Marzano (about 16)*
Fresh basil *to taste*
Salt *to taste*

Rinse tomatoes, remove stems, and cut very shallow Xs into bottoms. Bring a large pot of water to a boil. Blanch tomatoes in boiling water for 30 seconds. Remove tomatoes and put them in a bowl of ice water. When cool, peel the tomatoes (seeding is optional). Cut tomatoes in half, sprinkle them with salt, and let them drain in a colander. Dice tomatoes and follow canning instructions.

How to Sterilize Jars and Containers
Partially fill a boiling-water canner with hot water. Place clean canning jars into the canner. Cover and bring water to a boil over high heat. Boil for at least 10 minutes (or up to 30 minutes, depending on canner size). Five minutes before you are ready to fill the jars, place lids in boiling water according to manufacturer's directions.

Canning Instructions
Ladle preserves into the sterilized canning jars, leaving 1 inch of headroom. Be sure there are no air bubbles in the jar. Wipe the rims, put on the lids, and screw on the bands fingertip tight.

Put jars in a large pot fitted with a canning rack. Add enough water to cover the jars by 2 to 3 inches. Bring the water to a boil over high heat, then lower the heat to maintain a rolling boil. Boil jars for 40 minutes. Be sure the jars are covered with water the entire time. Turn off the heat. Wait 5 minutes and then use a jar lifter to transfer jars to a rack or towel and let cool. If the seal is not tight, refrigerate the jar and use within 10 days. If seal is tight, date jars and store them in a cool, dry place. The preserves will keep, unopened and at room temperature, for up to 1 year. After opening, store in refrigerator and use within 10 days.

MELON SALSA

Preparation time: 12 minutes   Cooking time: 20 minutes   Difficulty: easy

6 SERVINGS

*1 small **cantaloupe melon**, or about 1 lb. (500 g)*
*1/2 cup (100 ml) **sweet wine** (preferably a Muscat)*
*1/4 cup (50 g) **sugar***
*Juice and grated zest of 1 **lemon***
*1 tbsp. (15 g) **unsalted butter***
*1 tsp. (3 g) **cornstarch** or all-purpose flour*

Cut melon in half, then peel, seed, and cut into medium pieces.
In a saucepan, simmer melon for 10 minutes with sweet wine and sugar, stirring occasionally. Remove from heat and add the lemon juice, grated zest, butter, and flour or cornstarch. Stir.
On low heat, bring melon mixture to a boil and let it thicken slowly for 10 minutes, stirring frequently.
When cooked, remove mixture from pan, place it in a heatproof bowl, and let it cool completely. Store in refrigerator in an airtight container.
Serve cold with a pork tenderloin or a grilled fish such as swordfish.

CHERRY SAUCE

Preparation time: 20 minutes   Cooking time: 25 minutes   Difficulty: easy

6 SERVINGS

*11 oz. (300 g) sweet **cherries***
*1/2 cup (125 ml) **water***
*1/3 cup (60g) **sugar***
*2 tbsp. (25 ml) **cherry brandy***
*1 tbsp. (15g) **unsalted butter***
*2 tbsp. (20g) **all-purpose flour***
*Pinch of **nutmeg***

Rinse, dry, and pit the cherries. In a medium saucepan over medium heat, cook
the cherries with the water, sugar, and cherry brandy until they are pulpy, then
remove the pan from heat. To the cherry mixture, add butter, flour, and nutmeg,
and purée together in a bowl or blend in a blender.
Pour the mixture into a saucepan and let it thicken on low heat,
stirring to avoid lumps.
When the sauce is velvety, remove from heat and let it cool until it reaches room
temperature. Refrigerate sauce.
Serve cold.
Cherry sauce pairs nicely with duck and pork.

QUINCE SAUCE

Preparation time: 12 minutes   Cooking time: 5 minutes   Difficulty: easy

6 SERVINGS

1/2 cup (100 ml) **sweet wine** (preferably a Muscat)
1 tbsp. **quince jelly**
1/2 cup (50 g) **raisins**
1/4 cup (25 g) **hazelnuts**
1/4 cup (25 g) chopped mixed **candied fruit**
1 tbsp. plus 1 tsp. (20 ml) **apple cider vinegar**
Pepper to taste

Soak raisins in a bowl of warm water for 10 minutes, then drain. Meanwhile, put the wine in a saucepan and slowly bring to a boil. Let wine boil for 30 seconds, then add quince jelly, raisins, hazelnuts, candied fruit, vinegar and pepper. Bring the mixture to a boil, remove from heat, and let cool completely. Transfer sauce to an airtight container and refrigerate until ready to serve.
The sauce should be served cold. It pairs very well with cheese and with poultry.

PRESERVES:

Italian cuisine uses a wealth of excellent produce—fresh when it is in season, and preserved to enjoy when the season has ended. A dizzying array of sweet and savory preserves bursts with the flavors of abundant gardens and memories of warm summer days even during the coldest months.

There is nothing better than a homemade preserve to supply a personal, unique touch to a dish or an occasion—an aromatic limoncello served after a meal, sun-dried tomatoes in oil to enhance an appetizer, marmalade with a slice of buttered toast for breakfast. Preserves are that little extra that makes the difference. A tart with raspberry jam can be delicious, but if the raspberries are those you collected during a walk in the mountains with friends, the fruit that you washed, dried, cooked and lovingly cared for to make jam, the tart will have a special emotional resonance.

Foods have been preserved since ancient times, as there has always been a need to ensure edibles throughout the year. This need led to increasingly advanced techniques and culinary finesse. If, as the saying suggests, it is beneficial to "make a virtue out of necessity," the story of canned goods proves you can also make necessity enjoyable. Since the Middle Ages, Italians have been preparing sweet conserves and jams, thanks to the cultivation of sugar cane (brought to Sicily by the Arabs in the eighth century) and the Venetian monopoly of the sugar trade. While these jams were originally intended for the privileged classes, they eventually trickled down to the lower classes as sugar was extracted from sugar beets and more readily available.

The most widely used preservation method involves heat sterilization, which only works if done properly and carefully: the glass jars must be well sealed and given enough space to avoid touching each other. They then need to be stored in a cool, dry, dark place (see sterilization and canning instructions on page 34). Other methods for preserving foods involve reducing the water content through drying and salting, or by adding sugar or vinegar.

A preserved product, of course, will have a different flavor, texture and color from a fresh one, but as history has shown, it can be just as delicious.

SALT-PACKED ANCHOVIES

Preparation time: 2 hours plus 1 month to cure Difficulty: easy

4 SERVINGS

4 1/2 lbs (2 kg) **fresh anchovies**
2 lbs (1 kg) **coarse salt**

Scale the anchovies (using a butter knife, scrape backward, from tail to head). Rinse anchovies once they are scaled, and place in a bowl of ice water until ready to continue cleaning.

To remove the heads, use a sharp knife to make a cut at an angle behind the anchovy's head. Make another diagonal cut from the middle of the first cut to the vent, just in front of the bottom fin. Remove all the innards. Rinse the anchovies and pat them dry. Anchovies that will be packed in salt should not be damp, as this would compromise the preservation process.

Spread a layer of coarse salt in the bottom of a large, wide glass container that has been thoroughly cleaned and completely dried. Arrange a layer of anchovies, placing them head to tail to maximize the space.

Top them with another layer of salt, 1/3 to 1/2 inch (1 cm) high.

Continue with another layer of anchovies, perpendicular to the previous layer. Continue until all the anchovies have been used. Cover them with plenty of salt, leaving no empty space between anchovies.

Place a cover of glass or wood (with a diameter slightly smaller than that of the container) on top of the anchovies. Then put a weight of about 4 1/2 lbs (2 kg) on top of the cover so the fish are well compressed.

Keep the anchovies in a cool, dark, dry place for at least 30 days to cure.

SWEET-AND-SOUR ONIONS

Preparation time: 30 minutes   Cooking time: 25 minutes   Difficulty: easy

4 SERVINGS

14 oz. (400 g) **pearl onions**
3 1/2 tbsp. (50 ml) **extra-virgin olive oil**
2 1/2 tbsp. (30 g) **sugar**
5 1/2 tbsp. (80 ml) **balsamic vinegar**
3 **bay leaves**
Salt *to taste*

Peel, clean and rinse the onions. Bring a pot of salted water to a boil, then blanch the onions for a few seconds and drain. Heat the oil in a skillet and add the onions. Sauté for a few minutes, then add the sugar. When the sugar begins to brown, splash with the balsamic vinegar and add the bay leaves. Cook until the onions are soft and the cooking juices have a syrupy consistency (if necessary, add a few tablespoons of water).
Refrigerate sweet-and-sour onions in a jar with a tight-fitting lid. Remove bay leaves before serving.
Serve as an accompaniment to poultry and fish.

COGNÀ
(PIEDMONTESE MUSTARD)

Preparation time: 20 minutes   Cooking time: 4 hours   Difficulty: easy

4 SERVINGS

10 1/2 quarts (10 l) **grape juice**
3 1/4 lbs. (1.5 kg) **quince**
3 1/4 lbs. (1.5 kg) **Bosc pears**
3 1/4 lbs. (1.5 kg) **peaches or prunes**
15 **fresh figs** (or 10 dried figs)
10 oz. (300 g) **walnut pieces**

10 oz. (300 g) **toasted hazelnuts**
10 oz. (300 g) **toasted almonds**
Zest of 3 **lemons**
10 to 12 **cloves**
2-in. (5-6 cm) **cinnamon stick**

In a large pot, boil the grape juice with the lemon zest and reduce to half.
Chop the fruit and add it in the following order: quince, pears, peaches, figs and
nuts. Place spices in a muslin or cheesecloth bag (or wrap in a square of the
fabric and tie off the end). Add the spice bag to the pot. Cook the sauce, stirring
frequently, for at least 4 hours, then pour it into sterilized glass jars
(see page 34 for sterilizing how-to).
Follow instructions on page 34 for boiling, cooling, and storing the mustard.
Serve with aged cheeses and roasted meats or a classic Piedmont
bollito misto (boiled meats).

PICKLED VEGETABLES
(GIARDINIERA)

Preparation time: 30 minutes   Cooking time: 15 minutes   Difficulty: easy

4 SERVINGS

1 lb. (500 g) **cauliflower**, or about 1 small head
10 oz. (300 g) **carrots**, or about 4 medium
5 oz. (150 g) **peppers**, or about 1 medium
7 oz. (200 g) **spring onions**

7 oz. (200 g) **cucumbers**, or about 1 medium
1 pint (500 ml) **white wine vinegar**
Fennel seeds (optional) to taste
2 1/2 tbsp. (30 g) **sugar**
Peppercorns to taste
Salt to taste

Prepare and wash all the vegetables. Leave the spring onions whole.
Cut the cauliflower into florets, slice the cucumber, cut the peppers into diamond shapes (you can even use a pasta cutter to make special shapes) and cut the carrots into sticks or another shape of your choice.
Boil the vinegar with the sugar in a saucepan, add a generous pinch of salt, a couple of peppercorns and some fennel seeds, if desired, to taste.
Boil the different types of vegetables separately in the vinegar, cooking them only to the point where they are still crisp. With a slotted spoon place the vegetables in sterilized glass jars (see sterilizing instructions on page 34), alternating them within the jar. Bring the liquid to a second boil and immediately pour it on the vegetables. Seal the glass jars and allow them to cool completely.
Refrigerate. Use the giardiniera within a week of preparing it.
To can the vegetables for use over time, follow the instructions on page 34 for sterilizing the jars.

EGGPLANT WITH VINEGAR

Preparation time: 30 minutes   Resting time: 4 hours   Difficulty: medium

4 SERVINGS

7 oz. (200 g) **eggplant**
1/2 cup plus 2 tbsp. (150 ml) **white vinegar**
1 clove **garlic**
4 **fresh mint leaves**
2 sprigs **fresh thyme**
1/2 cup plus 2 tbsp. (150 ml) **extra-virgin olive oil**
1 **red chile pepper**, *seeds and veins removed, chopped*
Salt *to taste*

Peel eggplant, remove ends, and rinse under cold water. Cut eggplant into strips about 1/4 inch (5 mm) thick and about 2 inches (5 cm) long, then put in a colander, salt it lightly and allow it to drain for about 30 minutes.

Discard liquid from pot and squeeze eggplants to remove excess liquid. Dry with paper towels, then place eggplant in a large bowl and cover completely with vinegar. Leave eggplant to rest for another 2 hours. Drain the vinegar, and squeeze eggplant strips to remove as much vinegar as possible. Put eggplant strips and the garlic clove in a sterilized glass canning jar with a tight-fitting lid. (For instructions on sterilizing jars, see page 34.)

Layer eggplant strips, adding chopped chile pepper, mint leaves and thyme to taste. After filling jar, carefully press down on eggplant strips, cover entirely with extra-virgin olive oil, and close jar. Let eggplant strips sit in jar for at least 2 days in refrigerator. Once jar is opened, eggplant should be consumed within 3 days. Serve eggplant with crusty bread, as an accompaniment to meats, or as a sandwich topping.

EGGPLANT MARINATED IN OIL

Preparation time: 1 hour   Difficulty: easy

4 SERVINGS

2 lbs. (1 kg) **eggplant**, *or about 2 medium*
2 cups (1/2 l) **white wine vinegar**
2 cloves **garlic**
2 tsp. (10 ml) **extra-virgin olive oil**
1 bunch **basil**
Oregano *(fresh or dried) to taste*
Salt *to taste*

Wash the eggplants and slice them 1/8-1/4 inch (5 mm) thick. Place the slices in a colander, sprinkle with salt, cover and let them drain for about 1 hour.
In a large pot, bring the vinegar to a boil, then add the eggplant slices for a few minutes.
Strain eggplant, squeezing out excess moisture, and lay the slices on a cloth to dry.
Arrange eggplant slices in glass jars with tight-fitting lids, along with a few basil leaves, sliced garlic and a pinch of oregano. Cover them with oil, let the mixture settle and top it off with oil if necessary. Let eggplant strips sit in jar in a cool, dark place for at least 2 days. Once jar is opened, eggplant should be consumed within 3 days.
To can eggplant for use in the longer term, see instructions on page 34.

CREMONA MUSTARD

Marinating time: 5 days   Cooking time: 55 minutes   Difficulty: medium

4 SERVINGS

2 lbs. (1 kg) **mixed fruit** *(mandarin oranges, pears, tart apples, cherries)*
2 1/2 cups (500 g) **sugar**
5-10 drops/lb. (10-20 drops/kg) **mustard essence** *or 2 oz. mustard powder diluted
in 1/4 cup* **white wine vinegar**

Peel and dice the fruit, place it in a bowl and sprinkle with sugar.
Macerate at room temperature for about 24 hours. Drain the juice that has
formed, pour it into a saucepan and boil for about 10 minutes, then pour
it back over the fruit.
Leave fruit and juice to macerate for another 24 hours. Each day, repeat the
process above for a total of 5 days. On the last day, boil all the ingredients
(including the fruit) for 5 minutes.
Add the mustard essence or diluted mustard powder. Let cool completely.
Pour the resulting mustard into canning jars with tight-fitting lids. Seal the jars
and store in a cool, dry place. Refrigerate jars after opening.
Serve as an accompaniment to braised beef and pork.

MANTUA MUSTARD

Marinating time: 3 days   *Cooking time: 25 minutes*   *Difficulty: easy*

4 SERVINGS

2 lbs. (1 kg) **quince**, *or tart apples*
2 1/2 cups (400 g) **sugar**
5-10 drops/lb. (10-20 drops/kg) **mustard essence** *or 2 oz. mustard powder diluted in 1/4 cup* **white wine vinegar**

Peel and slice the apples, place them in a bowl and sprinkle with sugar.
Let them macerate for about 24 hours. Drain the juice that has formed, pour it into a small saucepan and boil for about 10 minutes, then pour it back over the apples. Let macerate for another 24 hours and repeat the process.
Again let the apples macerate for another 24 hours and then boil the mixture (including the apples) for 5 minutes.
Add the mustard essence or diluted mustard powder. Pour the resulting mustard into canning jars with tight-fitting lids (follow instructions on page 34 for sterilizing jars and canning for long-term storage). Seal the jars and store in a cool, dry place. Refrigerate jars after opening.
Serve as an accompaniment to braised beef and pork.

SUN-DRIED TOMATOES IN OIL

Preparation time: 20 minutes   Cooking time: 5 minutes   Difficulty: easy

4 SERVINGS

10 oz. (300 g) **sun-dried tomatoes**
3/4 cup plus 1 1/2 tbsp. (200 ml) **water**
3/4 cup plus 1 1/2 tbsp. (200 ml) **white wine**
1/2 cup (100 ml) **wine vinegar**
4 tsp. (15 g) **sugar**
1 **bay leaf**
1 tsp. **ground pepper**
1 tsp. **ground coriander**
3 tsp. (20 g) **salt**
3 1/2 tbsp. (50 ml) **extra-virgin olive oil**

Put all the ingredients except the tomatoes and oil in a pan.
Bring mixture to a boil and add the tomatoes.
Simmer for 5 minutes, then drain the tomatoes, dry with a cloth, and let cool completely. Put them in glass canning jars with tight-fitting lids.
Cover with extra-virgin olive oil and seal the jars.
Store them in a cool, dark place, and, once opened, refrigerate.
To can the tomatoes for use in the longer term, follow the instructions on page 34 for sterilizing the jars and canning the tomatoes.

CARROT AND ORANGE JAM

Preparation time: 15 minutes   Resting time: 3-12 hours
Cooking time: 30 minutes   Difficulty: easy

MAKES ABOUT TWO 18 OZ. (500 G) JARS

1 lb. (500 g) **carrots**
2 cups (400 g) **sugar**
Juice from 1 **lemon**
1/2 cup plus 2 tbsp. (150 ml) **orange juice**
Zest from 1 **orange**

Peel and grate carrots. Put them in a glass or stainless-steel bowl, stir in sugar, cover and refrigerate for several hours (preferably overnight).
Put carrot mixture in a medium saucepan, add lemon and orange juices and the orange zest, and cook on low heat, stirring constantly, for about 30 minutes.
To see if jam has reached its set point, dip a cool metal spoon into the simmering mixture and lift the spoon out of the steam so the syrup runs off the side. When the mixture first starts to boil, the drops will be light and syrupy. As the syrup continues to boil, the drops will become heavier and will drop off the spoon two at a time. When the two drops form together and "sheet" off the spoon, the set point has been reached.
Follow instructions on page 34 for sterilizing canning jars and canning the preserves.

CHERRY JAM

Preparation time: 35 minutes   Cooking time: 30 minutes
Resting time: 3-12 hours   Difficulty: easy

MAKES ABOUT TWO 12-OZ. (350 G) JARS

1 3/4 lb. (750 g) **cherries**
1 cup (200 g) **sugar**

Wash and dry cherries, remove stems, and pit the fruit. Place cherries in a glass or stainless-steel bowl, add sugar, stir together, and refrigerate for several hours (preferably overnight).

Put cherry mixture in a medium saucepan and cook on low heat, stirring constantly, for about 30 minutes.

To see if jam has reached its set point, dip a cool metal spoon into the simmering mixture and lift the spoon out of the steam so the syrup runs off the side. When the mixture first starts to boil, the drops will be light and syrupy. As the syrup continues to boil, the drops will become heavier and will drop off the spoon two at a time. When the two drops form together and "sheet" off the spoon, the set point has been reached.

If you prefer a smoother jam, pass it through a food mill or purée in a blender. Follow instructions on page 34 for sterilizing canning jars and canning the jam.
Cherry jam pairs well with cheese.

PUMPKIN JAM

Preparation time: 1 hour   Cooking time: 5 minutes
Resting time: 1 hour   Difficulty: easy

MAKES ABOUT FOUR 12-OZ. (350 G) JARS

3 1/2 lbs. (1.5 kg) **whole pumpkin** *(any variety)*
3 1/2 cups (700 g) **brown sugar**
1/3 cup (70 g) **water**
1/2 juice of **lemon**

Wash pumpkin, cut into small pieces and remove seeds. Using a basket steamer,
steam pumpkin for about 30 minutes or until it is tender (you can also use a
pressure cooker for 3 to 5 minutes).
Allow pumpkin to cool, then scrape flesh from shell and blend in a food mill
or food processor. Measure out 3 cups (750 grams) into a bowl, add sugar,
and let stand for 1 hour.
Bring pumpkin mixture to a boil over medium heat, and add lemon juice.
Boil for 5 minutes.
Follow instructions on page 34 for sterilizing canning jars and canning the jam.

STRAWBERRY PRESERVES

Preparation time: 10 minutes   Cooking time: 30 minutes   Difficulty: easy

4 SERVINGS

2 lbs. (1 kg) **strawberries**
4 cups (800 g) **sugar**
1 tbsp. (15 ml) **lemon juice**

Clean and rinse the strawberries and set them out to dry on a clean kitchen towel. Cut them into small pieces and put them in a large pot with the sugar and lemon juice and bring to a boil. Cook over medium heat for 30 minutes, stirring frequently.

To see if jam has reached its set point, dip a cool metal spoon into the simmering mixture and lift the spoon out of the steam so the syrup runs off the side. When the mixture first starts to boil, the drops will be light and syrupy. As the syrup continues to boil, the drops will become heavier and will drop off the spoon two at a time. When the two drops form together and "sheet" off the spoon, the set point has been reached.

Follow instructions on page 34 for sterilizing jars and canning the jam.

GREEN TOMATO CHUTNEY

Preparation time: 15 minutes   Resting time: 12 hours
Cooking time: 45 minutes   Difficulty: easy

4 SERVINGS

1 lb. (500 g) **green tomatoes**
5 oz. (150 g) **turbinado (cane) sugar**
1 **lemon**

Wash and dry the tomatoes, halve and remove the seeds and cut into strips about 1/4 in (6 mm) wide. Put in a glass bowl with the sugar, cover with plastic wrap and let macerate for 24 hours at room temperature.

The next day, zest and juice the lemon.

Pour the tomato mixture into a pan. Add the lemon juice and grated lemon zest. Cook for about 45 minutes, stirring frequently, until the mixture has the consistency of thick jam.

Pour the chutney into a glass jar with a tight-fitting lid if using immediately. Follow instructions on page 34 for sterilizing canning jars and canning the chutney, for long-term storage.

Tomato chutney is delicious paired with chicken, beef, or pork. It also makes a great sandwich spread, especially with cheese.

LEMON CREAM

Preparation time: 15 minutes   Cooking time: 5 minutes   Difficulty: medium

4-6 SERVINGS

2 tsp. (10 ml) **lemon juice**, plus zest of 1/2 lemon, grated
6 tbsp. (85 g) **unsalted butter**
1 cup (125 g) **confectioners' sugar**
4 **egg yolks**
2 tbsp. (20 g) **cornstarch, sifted**

In a saucepan, boil lemon juice and zest with butter and half the sugar.
Let boil for 10 minutes, stirring constantly.
In a bowl, beat egg yolks with the remaining sugar, then add sifted cornstarch.
Add to the lemon mixture, and bring to a boil, stirring well. Cook for 5 minutes.
Let cool.
Enjoy the tart-sweet cream as a dessert on its own, with ice cream or fresh berries, or spread on scones.

GIANDUIA CREAM SPREAD

Preparation time: 25 minutes   Difficulty: easy

MAKES ABOUT 1 1/2 CUPS

4 1/2 oz. (125 g) **dark chocolate**
4 1/2 oz. (125 g) **milk chocolate**
1/3 cup (100 g) **hazelnut paste**
3 tbsp. (50 ml) **light extra-virgin olive oil**

Put dark chocolate and milk chocolate in separate heatproof bowls and place in a bain-marie (hot-water bath) until chocolate is melted. (You can also melt the chocolate in the microwave oven.)

Stir together both chocolates and the hazelnut paste. Add the extra-virgin olive oil (prefably a light, delicate variety), stirring well until the mixture is warmed through. However, do not let it begin to thicken.

Allow the gianduia cream to cool. Pour into a glass jar with a tight-fitting lid, or another airtight container. (For instructions on sterilizing jars and how to can, see page 34.)

Store in a cool, dry place for up to 1 month.

Spread gianduia on croissants, crêpes, French toast and other baked goods.

MANDARIN JELLY

Preparation time: 15 minutes   Resting time: 2 hours   Difficulty: easy

4–6 SERVINGS

5 **gelatin sheets**, *about 1/2 oz. (12.5 g)*
1/2 cup **warm water**
1 cup (200 g) **sugar**
1 1/2 cups (360 g) **tangerine juice** *or orange juice*
Juice of 2 **lemons**
4 oz. **rum**
Mandarin oranges, *for garnish (optional)*

Soak the gelatin in warm water, then squeeze out excess liquid. In a saucepan, cook the gelatin with the sugar until it dissolves, taking care not to let it boil or it will become bitter.
Pour into a wet gelatin mold, along with the tangerine and lemon juices and the rum. Refrigerate for 2 hours.
Turn out onto a serving plate. Garnish with slices of mandarin orange.

ORANGE MARMALADE

Preparation time: 20 minutes   Cooking time: 45 minutes
Resting time: 8-10 hours   Difficulty: easy

MAKES ABOUT THREE 2-LB. (1 KG) JARS

2 lbs. (1 kg) **whole thin-skinned oranges**, *such as blood oranges (preferably organic)*
2 lbs. (1 kg) **sugar**
Juice from 2 lbs. (1 kg) **whole lemons**

Carefully wash oranges. Peel half the oranges and slice thinly. Slice remaining oranges with peels left on.

Place slices in a container or large serving dish, alternating layers of oranges with sugar, until all ingredients have been used. Let the mixture macerate for 8 to 10 hours at room temperature, then add the lemon juice and cook in a large saucepan over medium heat, taking care to occasionally skim the foam.

Stir often until the jam is so dense that it does not slide off a wooden spatula.

Follow instructions on page 34 for sterilizing jars and canning the marmalade.

PEARS IN SYRUP

Preparation time: 1 hour 25 minutes   Cooking time: 5 minutes
Sterilization: 30 minutes   Difficulty: easy

MAKES ABOUT TWO 28-OZ. (800 G) JARS

3 1/4 lbs. (1 kg) **pears** *(preferably Abate, if available, or Bartlett)*
2 cups (400 g) **sugar**
1/4 cup (50 g) **water**
1 **vanilla bean**
Zest of 1 **lemon**
2 **cloves**

Peel pears, leaving stems attached.
Prepare the syrup: Melt sugar and water in a saucepan, add the vanilla bean
sliced lengthwise, the lemon zest, and cloves, and boil for 3 to 4 minutes, then
remove pan from heat.
Place pears in the syrup and cook for 5 minutes, then remove from heat.
Arrange pears in airtight jars (follow following instructions on page 34 for
sterilizing jars), cover with boiling syrup, and seal. Then follow instructions for
canning on page 34.

PEACHES IN SYRUP

Preparation time: 2 hours   *Difficulty: easy*

4 SERVINGS

2 lbs. (1 kg) **firm yellow peaches**
2 cups (400 g) **sugar**
1 **vanilla bean**
Zest of 1 **lemon**
2 **cloves**
2 1/2 cups (600 ml) **water**

Bring a pot of water to a boil and place peaches in boiling water for 1 minute. Remove them with a slotted spoon and immediately put them in an ice-water bath so the skin will be easier to remove. Cut them in half, remove the pits, and lay them on a clean kitchen towel to dry.

In the meantime, make the syrup. Cut the lemon zest into thin strips. Dissolve the sugar in the water. Let it boil for a few minutes with the vanilla, strips of lemon zest, and the cloves. Remove from heat. Arrange the peaches in sterilized glass jars, following instructions on page 34 for sterilizing jars), cover with boiling syrup, and seal. Follow instructions for canning on page 34, to complete the canning.

LIMONCELLO

Preparation time: 1 hour   Resting time: 14 days plus 1 month   Difficulty: easy

4 SERVINGS

6 **organic lemons** (preferably Sorrento)
2 cups (0.5 l) **180-proof alcohol,** such as Everclear
1 cup (250 ml) **water**
1 cup plus 2 tbsp. (225 g) **sugar**

Rinse and dry the lemons. Use a vegetable peeler to remove the zest. Put the
pieces of zest in a sterilized jar with a tight-fitting lid (see page 34 for instructions
on sterilizing jars and bottles) and cover them completely with the alcohol. Keep
it in a cool, dark place for 2 weeks, shaking it every day to mix well.
Make the syrup: In a saucepan, bring the water to a boil and dissolve the sugar
in it. Let it boil for 2 to 3 minutes. Let it cool and add it to the alcohol and zest.
Mix well and strain it with cheesecloth. Pour it into bottles and store
it in a cool, dark place for at least 1 month before consuming it.
Keep the limoncello in the freezer and serve it ice cold.

EGG LIQUEUR

Preparation time: 15 minutes   Cooking time: 10 minutes
Resting time: 24 hours   Difficulty: easy

MAKES ABOUT THREE CUPS (3/4 L)

5 *egg yolks*
1 1/4 cups (250 g) *cane sugar*
5 oz. (150 ml) *milk*
1 cup (250 ml) *Marsala wine*
3 1/2 tbsp. (50 ml) ***80-proof alcohol**, such as Everclear*
1/2 *vanilla bean, split lengthwise*

Beat the egg yolks and sugar in a saucepan. In another pan, boil the milk, then add it to the egg-yolk mixture together with the Marsala and the vanilla bean. Cook over low heat (or in a hot-water bath), whisking constantly until the mixture reaches a temperature of 185°F (85°C) on an instant-read thermometer. Let cool, then add the alcohol. Pour the mixture into a bottle and seal carefully. (See instructions on sterilizing containers on page 34.) Let mature in the refrigerator for 24 hours. Keep the egg liqueur in the refrigerator and shake the bottle well before serving.

WALNUT LIQUEUR

Preparation time: 10 minutes   Resting time: 40 days   Difficulty: easy

4 SERVINGS

12 **green walnuts** *in their shells*
4 1/4 cups (1 l) **red wine**
1 1/4 cups (250 g) **sugar**
1 cup (250 ml) **180-proof alcohol**, *such as Everclear*
1 *pinch of* **cinnamon**
1 **clove**
Zest from 1/4 **lemon** *(excluding pith)*

Cut the walnuts into quarters and combine them with the other ingredients in a sterilized jar with a tight-fitting lid. (Follow instructions for sterilizing containers on page 34.) Keep liqueur in a cool, dark place for 40 days.
When 40 days have passed, filter the liqueur with cheesecloth and store it in well-sealed bottles. (For instructions on sterilizing bottles, see page 34.)

INGREDIENTS INDEX

PHOTO CREDITS

All photographs are by ACADEMIA BARILLA except the following:
page 6, 95 ©123RF

Original edition © 2013 by De Agostini Libri S.p.A.

The Taunton Press
Inspiration for hands-on living®

The Taunton Press, Inc.
63 South Main Street
PO Box 5506, Newtown, CT 06470-5506
e-mail: tp@taunton.com

Translations:
Catherine Howard - Mary Doyle - John Venerella - Free z'be, Paris
Salvatore Ciolfi - Rosetta Translations SARL - Rosetta Translations SARL

LIBRARY OF CONGRESS CATALOGING-IN-PUBLICATION DATA IN PROGRESS
ISBN: 978-1-62710-055-7

Printed in China
10 9 8 7 6 5 4 3 2 1